The Practical
Tao Te Ching
of Lao-zi

The Practical
Tao Te Ching
of Lao-zi

Rational Meditations on Non-duality,
Impermanence, Wu-wei (non-striving), Nature
and Naturalness, and Virtue

陳
志
強

Mushin Press

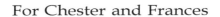

For Chester and Frances

Contents

Note: Each chapter has been given a brief "title" as a convenience so that the reader has a general idea of the topic that is addressed.

INTRODUCTION

The Tao Te Ching 道德經 (or the more modern spelling: Dao de Jing), is said to be one of the most translated texts in the world, second to only the Bible.[1] So, Why is another translated version of the Tao Te Ching necessary? you might ask.

An American friend had been reading a translation of the Tao Te Ching and commented that it seemed too esoteric and ambiguous to be of much value.

"Well, if you first understand the basic Taoist principles, then it's easier to understand," I suggested.

"But how can you know the basic principles if you haven't read the texts?"

"Hmm, that's an excellent question."

I first became familiar with Taoist thought when I was living in Taiwan. My conversations with Taiwanese friends would regularly lead to the names Lao-zi and Zhuang-zi of Taoist renown. The Taoist stories my friends shared with me were often not only entertaining but also insightful and thought-provoking. My interest in the Tao was thus inspired.

My initial attempts at understanding the Tao Te Ching came through English translations written by Chinese academics and scholars. I found them, however, as my friend may attest, tending toward the mystical and abstruse, and not written in a style of English prose I found so familiar or easily comprehensible. I suppose I could have sat there ruminating and meditating on it all, but

[1] Alan Chan, *Laozi*, Edward N. Zalta (ed.), The Stanford Encyclopedia of Philosophy (Spring 2014 Edition), http://plato.stanford.edu/entries/laozi/(retrieved 01/05/2015)

I did not. Instead, I turned to the translated works of Western academics. Focused on political and historical context, scholarly and dry, these versions were not especially poetic, inspiring, or enlightening (or enjoyable to read for that matter). The third commonly found approach to translating the Tao Te Ching is the poetic one, and this is where I ended up, eventually coming upon a popular English version that appeared relatively lucid and seemingly infused with insight and wisdom. Because why is one inspired to contemplate a writing such as the Tao Te Ching anyway, if it is it not to seek some truth about the nature of our humanity, our existential reality, our human condition?

After several years of living in Taiwan and studying Chinese, I decided one day to read a Chinese version of the Tao Te Ching and compare it to the various English translations I had earlier read. Ah, now, I kind of got it. The "it" being not a clear, concise understanding of the meaning of the Tao Te Ching but rather why it read as such an enigmatic piece of writing. Moreover, when I reviewed the popular English version (the one I had previously considered lucid and insightful) against the Chinese version, I found the English translation to have some verses that were completely missing and others that seemed to be created totally out of whole cloth. Further research revealed that this Western author had created his popularly-received interpretation by reading the English translations of others, adding his own mystical and spiritual tendencies, and stirring it all into a poetic brew of what he imagined the Taoist notions to be. Of course, every person is bound to have his or her own interpretations, but if one is not elucidating on a document from its original source, why claim any expositions as a translation? Why not call the work something more appropriate such as, "The Tao of Mr. or Ms. XYZ." Not so mystical-sounding, nor marketable, I admit.

If I were going to genuinely contemplate this text called the Tao Te Ching, then, I preferred to consider an accurate representation of it, not someone's personally contrived imaginings of it.

This returned me to translations by academics and scholars. While it seemed more likely I would be able to find a clear and concise interpretation of the Tao Te Ching from one who had a thorough knowledge of the Chinese language and culture, I found this was not necessarily so.

Enigma and Ambiguity

The fact that scholars still debate whether 老子—Lao-zi (or Lau Tzu), the stated author of the Tao Te Ching, is a true historical figure, a legendary figure, or as is often argued: that the Tao Te Ching is derived from the writings of various authors[2], does not bode well for those depending on academia for an understanding of the Tao Te Ching.

Regardless of one's level of scholarship, the difficulty accurately interpreting a classical Chinese text begins with the structure of the Chinese language. Here are four reasons traditional Chinese texts are not easily translated:

1. Chinese, traditionally, has no punctuation;
2. a single Chinese character can have a variety of meanings;
3. pronoun reference errors are commonly encountered;
4. Chinese writing often makes references to standard literary works of the era.

1. Punctuation, or the Lack Thereof

What is the value of punctuation? Do we really need those marks and typographic symbols to clearly convey meaning in a printed or written text? Well, yes, as a matter of fact, we do. As the writer and journalist Lynne Truss wittily points out in her popular book *Eats, Shoots & Leaves: The Zero Tolerance Approach to Punctuation*, punctua-

[2] Alan Chan, *Laozi*, Edward N. Zalta (ed.), The Stanford Encyclopedia of Philosophy (Spring 2014 Edition), http://plato.stanford.edu/entries/laozi/(retrieved 01/05/2015)

tion is vital to precise expression and understanding of the written word. Compare how punctuation affects the meaning of the following sentences:

1. A woman, without her man, is nothing.
2. A woman: without her, man is nothing.[3]

And how about the joke that inspires the title of Ms. Truss' book:

A panda walks into a café. He orders a sandwich, eats it, then draws a gun and fires two shots in the air.

"Why?" asks the confused waiter, as the panda makes towards the exit. The panda produces a badly punctuated wildlife manual and tosses it over his shoulder.

"I'm a panda," he says at the door. "Look it up."
The waiter turns to the relevant entry and, sure enough, finds an explanation.

"Panda. Large black-and-white bear-like mammal, native to China. Eats, shoots and leaves."[4]

(Compare the last sentence to the comma-less: "Eats [bamboo] shoots and leaves.")

Punctuation markings and symbols are a modern addition to the written Chinese language; in the past, there were none. In previous days, the reader of a Chinese text determined for oneself where one phrase ended and another began, where one sentence concluded and another initiated. A lack of punctuation markings and symbols, as the above examples demonstrate, can result in a single text being interpreted in any number of ways.

2. One word and a range of possibilities

[3] Lynne Truss, *Eats, Shoots & Leaves*, Illustrated Edition (Gotham Books, 2003) 23
[4] Lynne Truss, *Eats, Shoots & Leaves*, Illustrated Edition (Gotham Books, 2003)

As with most languages, a single word might be used to express a variety of meanings. The Chinese word 故 (gù), for example, can be used to mean: (n.) *acquaintance, cause, friend, happening, instance, reason*; (v.) *to die*; (adv.) *therefore, hence, intentionally*; or (adj.) *old, deceased*—and so on. Imagine a line of ten characters with each word having such a vast array of possible definitions and, therefore, interpretations.

3. The Pronoun Reference Error

In the Chinese language, pronouns are often not clearly differentiated (or the subject of a sentence is not clearly identified); the result can be a sentence which contains, what we call in English grammar, a "pronoun reference error." The following examples illustrate the ambiguity one encounters in these types of sentences.

- After Lauren gave Joanne the money, **she** left.
Who left? Lauren or Karen?

- The old man told the boy that **he** was being followed by thieves.
Who was being followed? The boy or the old man?

- Mike asked the young man what had happened to **his** car.
Whose car was it? Mike's or the young man's?

How can a person know with certainty whom the pronoun is referencing? One cannot. When sentences such as these appear in the Chinese language, the reader must reference the greater context of the writing before attempting to accurately interpret the meaning. Consider the first three verses from Chapter One of the *Tao Te Ching*.

1. 道可道，非常道。
名可名，非常名。

The Tao that can be told is not the eternal Tao.
The name that can be named is not the eternal name.

2. 無名天地之始。
   有名萬物之母。

The nameless is the beginning of heaven and earth.
The named is the mother of ten thousand things.

—Gia-fu Feng and Jane English

This translation, taken from Gia-fu Feng's and Jane English's *Lao Tsu: Tao Te Ching*[5], renders the first two verses consistently with the Chinese text. The following verse, however, becomes a bit problematic as it contains the undefined pronoun "其".

3. 故常無欲以觀**其**妙。
   常有欲以觀**其**徼。

Ever desireless, one can see the mystery.
Ever desiring, one can see the manifestations.

—Gia-fu Feng and Jane English

In Gia-fu Feng's and Jane English's version, this word "其" and its meaning is simply omitted. If one were to follow the Chinese text, this third verse could be translated to read something like this:

*Ever desireless, one can see **its/his/her/their/such** mystery.*
*Ever desiring, one can see **its/his/her/their/such** manifesta-*tions.

But, then, what is the "its/his/her/their/such" referring to, the "mystery" and "manifestations" of what, exactly? It is no

[5] Lao-zi translated by Gia-fu Feng and Jane English, *Lao Tsu: Tao Te Ching* (New York, Vintage Books, 1989)

wonder we can find myriad interpretations of the same verse (some more mystical-sounding than others):

Truly, "Only he that rids himself forever of desire can see the Secret Essences";
He that has never rid himself of desire can see only the Outcomes.

—Arthur Waley[6]

Hence always rid yourself of desires in order to observe its secrets;
But always allow yourself to have desires in order to observe its manifestations.

—D.C. Lau[7]

So, as ever hidden, we should look at its inner essence:
As always manifest, we should look at its outer aspects.

—John C. H. Wu[8]

Always passionless, thereby observe the subtle;
ever intent, thereby observe the apparent.

—Thomas Cleary[9]

So the unwanting soul
sees what's hidden,
and the ever-wanting soul
sees only what it wants.

—Ursula K. Le Guin[10]

Free from desire, you realize the mystery.
Caught in desire, you see only the manifestations.

—Stephen Mitchell[11]

[6] Arthur Waley, *The Way and its Power: A Study of the Tao Te Ching and its Place in Chinese Thought* (New York, Grove Press Inc.,1958)

[7] D.C. Lau, *Lao Tzu: Tao Te Ching* (New York, Penguin books, 1963)

[8] John C. H. Wu, *Tao Teh Ching* (Shambhala, 1990)

[9] Thomas Cleary, *The Essential Tao* (Harper San Francisco, 1991)

[10] Ursula K. Le Guin, *Lao Tzu: Tao Te Ching* (Shambhala Publications, 1997)

4. Referring to the Known

Chinese literature often includes metaphors and idioms that reference literary works or common historical or legendary events of the era. Without this familiarity, can a modern reader accurately interpret a group of words whose meaning is not literal?

The Philosophical Approach

Let us now return to our original enquiry: "Why is another version of the Tao Te Ching necessary?"

If one is curious whether this particular ancient Chinese text can offer, as I have suggested, some truth or insight into the nature of our humanity, our existential reality, our human condition, then a meaningful version of the Tao Te Ching should be one that:

- is a faithful representation of the original text;
- is lucid, rational, and common-sensical;
- is interpreted with a sensibility to the foundational philosophical Taoist principles of: 1) non-duality, 2) impermanence, 3) non-striving, and 4) naturalness. (Accordingly, one need first be familiar with these four basic principles of Taoist thought.)

1. Non-duality and 2. Impermanence

As I wrote in my previous book *The Buddha was not a Buddhist*, the fundamental concepts of non-duality and impermanence can be observed in the well-known Taoist symbol the taijitu (太極圖), more commonly referred to, in the West, as the "yin-yang symbol".

---

[11] Stephen Mitchell, *Tao Te Ching, Lao Tzu* (Frances Lincoln Limited, 1999)

Made up of a circle intersected with a curving line that separates the circle into halves, the white half represents the yáng (陽) state, and contains a small black dot. The other half is black and contains a small white dot; this half represents the yin (陰) state. Note that as the white yáng state reaches its peak, a black yin dot appears, leading to the birth of the black yin state, which then develops to its culmination, where the white yáng dot appears, leading back to the birth of the white yáng state.

Although the two halves may appear to represent opposites, they are not in opposition. One cannot exist without the other. The yin state and the yáng state are complementary and interdependent, two halves of an absolute whole. One does not have more value, is not more essential, is not more desired or avoided than the other. This is non-duality.

As the yin state arises from the yáng state and the yáng state arises from the yin state, we can observe a cycle of continuous transition and flux, the impermanence and ever-changing transformation of compounded phenomena, energy perpetually shifting from potential to kinetic to potential to kinetic ad infinitum, constantly evolving toward a state of the absolute—natural, balanced, effortless, and whole.

In the non-dualistic view, there is nothing desirable or undesirable, better or worse. Consider creation and destruction, or birth and death. Which is desirable? Which is to be avoided? The dualistic mind is drawn to what is "good" or "positive"—creation and birth—but imagine a world where nothing since the beginning of existence was ever destroyed; nothing ever died. You cannot. It would be chaos, and madness.

The non-dualistic mind recognizes creation arising from destruction and destruction the culmination of creation, birth arising from death and death the culmination of birth, then back again. These events are complementary and interdependent, effortless and fluid, forever maintaining an equilibrium, a non-governing homeostasis in the totality of the natural world.

The following story is adapted from a well-known Taoist parable about a farmer and his horse (塞翁失馬，焉知非福):

Near the northern border of China, there lived a farmer who owned a magnificent mare, acclaimed throughout the region. Not only beautiful and fast, the horse also pulled the farmer's plow through the fields.

One morning following a raging storm, the farmer went out to discover that the fence had been damaged and his prized mare had disappeared. His neighbor, always a bit envious of the farmer and his mare, heard the news and snickered. Quietly gratified, he dropped by to visit the farmer.

"I heard that your horse ran off," the neighbor called out. "What a shame."

To which the farmer replied, "Sure, I suppose so."

Puzzled, the neighbor walked off, *What do you mean you suppose so? It IS a shame that your horse ran off. Too bad for you.*

A few days later, the farmer looked out and spotted his mare back on the farm. Not only had his mare come home, but it had returned with three wild horses.

Upon hearing the news, the farmer's neighbor felt slightly irritated, *I can't believe it. He now has four horses.*

Once again, the neighbor went to pay the farmer a visit.

"I see your mare has returned and brought back with her three wild horses," he said to the farmer, adding with a note of insincerity, "That's great. You're the luckiest person in the village."

To which the farmer replied, "Sure, I suppose so."

Shaking his head, the neighbor returned home, muttering, "What do you mean you suppose so? You have the finest mare in the village and now three wild horses. I have one old, sick mare. You ARE lucky."

The next day the farmer's teen-aged son decided to train one of the wild horses. After choosing the most spirited of the three, he clambered atop, whereupon the untamed horse bucked and tossed the son into the air. Tumbling to the ground with an unsettling crack, the young man broke his leg.

The farmer's neighbor, predictably, returned to the farmer's house, "I'm so sorry to hear about your son. Now you'll have to do all your farm work by yourself. That's tough. I guess getting those three horses was bad luck after all."

To which the farmer replied, "Sure, I suppose so."

The neighbor could hardly disguise a smirk as he left, *You suppose so? You're nuts!*

Two weeks later, war broke out with the country to the north. Military officials and soldiers soon arrived at the village and began forcibly conscripting young men into the army. They came to the house of the farmer's neighbor and took away his eldest son. The neighbor then led them to the house of the farmer and shouted, "War has broken out! Military officials want to talk with you!" The farmer came out of his house, with his son hobbling behind him. The officials, seeing that the young man's leg was broken, turned away, saying, "He's useless. Let's go."

The neighbor stared at the farmer in disbelief. The farmer, glancing back at his neighbor, shrugged his shoulders and stepped back into his house.

I was once relating this story to a friend when he exclaimed, "Yes! Who's to know?"

Curious, I asked, "Who's to know what?"

"Who's to know if something is good or bad? You never know what might happen next."

Well, yes, while it may be true that we never know what will happen at any following moment, my friend overlooked the essence of this Taoist story. That is, the tale of the farmer and his horse embodies the view of non-duality: perceptions of good and bad do not exist independently of our conditioned thoughts. This goes beyond the notion of who is to know whether an occurrence is good or not good, bad or not bad, for presupposing that there exists a good or bad condition, in itself, indicates a dualistic world-view.

In the perception of the dualistic mind, the concept of good is to be desired and bad is to be avoided. This results in comparing and judging and separating, which invariably leads to conflict, the conflict of craving versus aversion. The manifestation of conflict then gives rise to the mental prattling of a grasping and fearful or dissatisfied dualistic mind, as in: "When this happens, my life will be perfect (good). If that happens, my life will be a mess (bad). He/she wants to be with me (good). He/she wants to break up with me (bad). That's what I want! I got it (good). I can't believe I didn't get it (bad)." And so on.

Being successful, being unsuccessful; being fortunate, being unfortunate; being recognized, being unknown; being unique, being ordinary; being important, being insignificant; being noticed, being ignored, all are concepts manufactured by the dualistic mind to be craved or avoided. The dualistic, conditioned mind is, ultimately, a source of mental torment, conflicted with the discontent from unsatiated craving and the anxiety arising from aversion.

3. Non-striving (wú wéi)

In the phenomena of the natural world (e.g., creation and destruction, birth and death) the characteristics of good and bad do not exist. In the non-dualistic mind, likewise, when something occurs, it is not perceived as this or that, not defined as good or bad. It simply is. There is only life, and living, dynamically, and in constant motion; living with events that are complementary and interdependent; living with the truth of impermanence and constant transformation; and, ultimately, living without the futile grasping of a craving, fear-filled, dogmatic mind. To live recognizing the true nature of non-duality leads to the third fundamental Taoist concept: 無爲 (wú wéi), often inaccurately interpreted as "non-action" or "non-doing". A more precise translation would be: non-striving or non-becoming.

To have no expectations nor desires nor ideas to be or to become, but to simply live, without the purposeful becoming of anything, is to allow life to occur according to the natural laws; one's behavior is thus effortless and uncontrived. This is nothing other than existing in a state of contentment—being, without mental conflict—emerging from a mind that has been liberated from the egoistic striving and craving to become something, which certainly does not mean to sit and do nothing. Not at all. An egoless mind, free of its dualistic cravings and aversions, is inspired to live without fear or despair or expectation or disappointment, because it matters not how a person feels about some circumstance. Conditions change. Constantly. Regardless, neither disheartened nor discouraged, one continues to live, and work, and learn, and be inspired, and create, and persevere. Another happening occurs, and he or she simply lives, without defining and comparing and judging and separating and craving—無爲 (wú wéi), non-striving or non-becoming—like a farmer and his horse.

4. Nature and Naturalness (zìrán)

Finally, there is the Taoist idea called 自然 (zìrán). A literal translation of these two characters is: "self hence, self so, self thus," therefore, this phrase is used to represent the concept of naturalness and nature, which is to describe a state of being that is unforced, unplanned, and uncontrived. To understand the nature of zìrán is to recognize the notions of non-duality and impermanence as the natural world constantly transforms toward a state of the absolute—natural, balanced, effortless, and whole. This returns us to the notion of wú wéi, non-striving, because not to strive means our actions are unforced, unplanned, and uncontrived, effortless and in harmony with nature, free of dualistic cravings and aversions; inspired, creative, fearless, free, and—content.

Meditate On It

Hopefully, after reading this translation of the Tao Te Ching, instead of thinking, *Gee, this seems kind of deep and meaningful, but . . . what the hell is he talking about?!*, you will come away with a better understanding of what Lao-zi had to teach.

第一章
道可道非常道名可名非常名無名天
地之始有名萬物之母故常無欲以觀
其妙常有欲以觀其徼此兩者同出而
異名同謂之玄玄之又玄眾妙之門

1

Knowledge and Truth

The tao that can describe the tao
is not the Tao.
Words that define concepts
do not define Truth.

That which is indefinable
is the essence of Heaven and Earth.
That which is definable
gives birth to the earthly realm.

Thus, have no mind for knowing,
and realize the wonder of the Tao;
have a mind for knowledge,
and discover the potential of the Tao.

No Mind and Mind,
arising from the same source,
convey the mysteries of the unknown,
which is the gateway to Truth.

Notes: A literal translation of the character " 名 " is normally "name," but what does this mean, exactly, "The name that can be named is not the eternal name,"[12]?

Consider what it means to "name" something. Is naming not simply creating a mental construct? Say "oak tree" and what arises in one's mind? An image, accompanied by more words and "names" of tree-related things: branches, leaves, trunk, bark, roots, and so on. In truth, what is an oak tree? Look outside and there it is, arising from the soil, but can that material and

12) Lao-zi translated by Gia-fu Feng and Jane English, *Lao Tsu: Tao Te Ching*

energetic form be given an objective definition? To a bird it may be shelter, with reflections of UV light; to a dog it may be a urinal, identified more by its scent than its muted (canine) coloring; to a caterpillar it may be a food source, known more by its texture and taste than its simple and indistinct (caterpillar) appearance, to a person it may be a source of shade or fuel, or raw material used for construction, and recognized by its large, strong and noble shape. The object we identify as an "oak tree" surely exists in the external world, but its definition is solely subjective, fabricated purely by the observer's perceptions.

To name and identify, to create knowledge, is to create mental constructs. The Tao, the Truth, is not a concept but rather what is: the existence of energy and material forms and their interrelationships in the external world. The mental constructs we create to define the world of our perceptions is not reality but rather are the names and concepts we use to fabricate the reality of our private mental universe; it is this that "gives birth to our earthly realm," our subjective perceptions of the world.

Although understanding the notions of Tao—non-duality, impermanence, non-striving, naturalness—helps to recognize the benefits of Tao, understanding does not lead to the being of it, which is only through action, the active living of Tao.

The conceptualizing of knowledge (the movement of the Mind) and the stilling of the mind (No Mind) have the same source: awareness, and both types of awareness in harmony can lead to realization of Truth.

第二章

天下皆知美之為美斯惡已皆知善之
為善斯不善已故有無相生難易相成
長短相較高下相傾音聲相和前後相
隨是以聖人處無為之事行不言之教
萬物作焉而不辭生而不有為而不恃
功成而弗居夫唯弗居是以不去

2

Non-dualistic thus Non-striving

Claim to know what is "beautiful"
and thus arises the "ugly".
Claim to know what is "good"
and thus arises the "bad".
Existence and non-existence are born as one.
"Difficult" and "effortless" mutually come into being.
"Long" and "short" define one another.
"High" is established by "low", and "low"
by "high".
Complementary sounds produce harmony.
"Before" and "after" are interdependent.

Thus, the Sage acts without intention,
teaches without words.

All nature continuously arises into existence:

> Born without claim;
> Living spontaneously;
> Thriving without accomplishment.

Without striving for accomplishment,
there is no loss;
there is no disappointment.

Notes: To mentally fabricate distinctions is to create dualistic notions that can lead to the striving for one condition and the avoiding of another, the origins of mental conflict, a divergence from the spontaneity and naturalness of the Tao. The non-dualistic, acting without intention, live in harmony with the natural world, the way of Tao. Thus, to live non-dualistically is to live without striving—wú wéi.

第三章

不尚賢使民不爭不貴難得之貨使民
不為盜不見可欲使民心不亂是以聖民
人之治虛其心實其腹弱其志強其骨
常使民無知無欲使夫智者不敢為也
為無為則無不治

3

Good Governance

Do not exalt the talented,
and people will not challenge one another.

Do not treasure precious objects,
and people will not become thieves.

Do not display objects of desire,
and people's minds will not become restive and
discontent.

Thus, the Sage governs by freeing people of desire
and providing for their necessities.
By tempering the people's egoistic ambition and
ensuring their wellbeing, the Sage inspires man's
unadulterated nature, free of craving, so that the
cunning dare not act.

Strive for nothing,
and all will be in order.

*Notes: Creating the dualistic distinctions that lead to craving and desire
results in individual and collective conflict and discontent, and, finally, disharmony.*

*Good governance provides the material necessities to sustain the people's
physical wellbeing and inspires the people to follow the Tao, which leads to the
people's mental and emotional wellbeing; thus the citizenry will live free of
conflict, not only among themselves but also with the natural environment.*

第四章

道沖而用之或不盈淵兮似萬物之宗
挫其銳解其紛和其光同其塵湛兮似
或存吾不知誰之子象帝之先

4

Origin of Tao

The Tao flows and is expended throughout,
never overflowing,
an immeasurable abyss
much like the origin of all things.

Blunting sharpness,
untangling confusion,
softening harshness;
one with the earth.

So profound,
can it exist?

I do not know this child,
who seems to have existed before the gods.

*Notes: Tao is the uncontrived and unintentioned (like a child) ordinary rhythms
and fluctuations of the natural world, a natural world that trends toward
homeostasis, a non-dualistic and constant state of flux and transformation.*

第五章
天地不仁以萬物為芻狗聖人不仁以
百姓為芻狗天地之間其猶橐籥乎虛
而不屈動而愈出多言數窮不如守中

5

Emptiness

Heaven and Earth are indifferent,
treating all without regard or concern (like straw dogs).

The Sage is similarly emotionless,
treating all without sentiment or bias.

May we compare the space between Heaven and Earth (suffused with the Tao) to that of a bellows?

> Empty but not incapable;
> Unrealized potential at the ready;
> Its action producing a restorative effect.

More ideas produce less understanding.

It is best to maintain the center.

Notes: In ancient China, a "straw dog" was a canine figure constructed of straw and used for ceremonial purposes. When the ritual was completed, the straw dog was discarded, without sentiment. Likewise, as elements of the Tao, all within the heavens and upon the earth fulfill their role in the non-dualistic cycling of energy and matter, and, finally, pass on, naturally, and without distinction.

*Ultimately, the accumulation and exposition of ideas and concepts result in greater difficulty stilling the mind into a consciousness of awareness, which leads one further from the Way, i.e., the active **being** of Tao.*

第六章
穀神不死是謂玄牝玄牝之門是謂天
地根緜緜若存用之不勤

6

Humility

The Spirit of the Valley does not die.
It is the subtle and indistinct feminine,
whose gateway is the birthplace of Heaven and
Earth.
Existing constant and unbroken,
it remains readily available.

Notes: The "Spirit of the Valley" represents the yin state, the feminine, humility. The Tao asserts that the yin state is always available to complement our yang nature—the human arrogance that causes us to drift from the homeostatic state of Tao.

第七章

天長地久天地所以能長且久者以其
不自生故能長生是以聖人後其身而
身先外其身而身存非以其無私邪故
能成其私

7

Selflessness and Self

Because they do not exist for themselves,
Heaven and Earth endure.

Likewise, the Sage is not preoccupied with
himself or herself
and lives outside of his or her own individuated
concerns.

Is it not because one has no self interest
that he or she can know the self?

Notes: To recognize the true nature of interconnectedness is to live in a state of homeostatic balance with the external world and the principles of Tao, which is constant, infinite, enduring. To recognize the true nature of our interconnectedness with the external world is to recognize that the idea of an individuated, autonomous self is an illusion.

第八章

上善若水水善利萬物而不爭處眾人之所惡故幾於道居善地心善淵與善仁言善信正善治事善能動善時夫唯不爭故無尤

8

Action without Intention

The most Virtuous are like water,
an element that benefits all earthly creatures.
Water gives life without striving or competing
and exists in places man finds unappealing.
It is much like the Tao.

A nice home is situated in the right location.

A good heart is boundless.

True relationships come from a kind heart.

Meaningful words arise from Truth.

Integrity makes good governance.

Having ability leads to handling affairs effectively.

Effective action is that which occurs at the
proper time.

One lives without striving or competing,
and is nothing in particular.

Notes: To recognize the Tao is to follow the natural laws without intention or
ambition or striving—wú wéi, like water.

第九章
持而盈之不如其已揣而梲之不可長
保金玉滿堂莫之能守富貴而驕自遺
其咎功成身退天之道也

9

Maintain the Center

Constant grasping to all that is desired leads to excess; thus, one can never know contentment.

Unbridled passion and intensity are impossible to maintain over an extended period.

A house brimming with treasures attracts the scrutiny of all.

When one is accomplished,
arrogance will cause his or her demise.

Complete the task,
step away,
and let it be.
This is the eternal Tao.

Notes: Act without the egoistic cravings and desires for constant satiation and sensation or social recognition and acknowledgment. Simply be, like the eternal Tao.

第十章

載營魄抱一能無離乎專氣致柔能嬰
兒乎滌除玄覽能無疵乎愛國治民能
無知乎天門開闔能為雌乎明白四達
能無為乎生之畜之生而不有為而不
恃長而不宰是謂玄德

10

A Virtuous Life

Can one maintain the mind and heart as a single spirit, without distraction?
Can one breathe as gently and softly as a newborn child?
Can one purify the mind and be free of delusion?
Can one love one's country and care for its people, without motive?
Ruling over the gates of Heaven, can one act with humility?
Can one understand the Infinite, without intention?

Give birth and nurture life.

Live without possessing.

Live, no longer acting dogmatic or tyrannical.

This is the mystery of Virtue.

Notes: Live freely and naturally and spontaneously, without intention, without the egoistic striving to attain or to acquire or to become.

第十一章

三十輻共一轂當其無有車之用埏埴

以為器當其無有器之用鑿戶牖以為

室當其無有室之用故有之以為利無

之以為用

11

The Value of What is Not

Thirty spokes meet at the hub of a wheel,
but it is the emptiness of the hub on which the cart
depends.

Clay is fashioned into a vessel,
but it is the empty hollow that makes the container
useful.

Doors and windows are built for a house,
but it is their open spaces that make the house
functional.

Therefore, use what you have to your advantage,
and realize the benefit of what you have not.

*Notes: To the non-dualistic, to have is no more or less desired than not to
have.*

第十二章

五色令人目盲五音令人耳聾五味令

人口爽馳騁畋獵令人心發狂難得之

貨令人行妨是以聖人為腹不為目故

去彼取此

12

Contentment

The five colors are able to blind you.
The five sounds are able to deafen you.
The five flavors are able to dull your palate.

Obsessive pursuit of desires
will make one go mad.

Possessions that are difficult to acquire
become obstacles in one's life.

Thus, the Sage acts to satisfy essential needs,
not to satiate cravings.
The Sage leaves the one
and gets the other.

Notes: Sensory stimulation taken to an extreme leads to harm or suffering or dullness.

To be free of craving or the wanting of something other is to be content. Once essential needs are secured—water, food, shelter, clothing, healthcare—contentment is attained by simply being satisfied with what is.

第十三章

寵辱若驚貴大患若身何謂寵辱若驚
寵為下得之若驚失之若驚是謂寵辱
若驚何謂貴大患若身吾所以有大患
者為吾有身及吾無身吾有何患故貴
以身為天下若可寄天下愛以身為天
下若可托天下

13

Self and Suffering

Both being esteemed and being insulted
provoke distress, much like giving one's "self"
great importance or great affliction.

How is it that both being esteemed and being
insulted brings agitation?
To be concerned with praise or aspersions is to be
preoccupied with gaining or losing the approval of
others.

How is it that attributing to the self both
significance and tragedy contributes to suffering?
Pride of and concern for the self arises anxiety and
self-doubt.

If the self vanishes,
what can know misery?

Therefore, value the world as you do your "self".
Surrender the love of the "self" to the world.
Love the earth as you would your "self",
and you are then able to care for all under the
heavens.

第十四章

視之不見名曰夷聽之不聞名曰希搏之不得名曰微此三者不可致詰故混而為一其上不皦其下不昧繩繩不可名復歸於無物是謂無狀之狀無物之象是謂惚恍迎之不見其首隨之不見其後執古之道以御今之有能知古始是謂道紀

14

Our Ancient Origins—Tao

Looked at but not seen,
it is the formless.
Listened to but not heard,
it is the inaudible.
Grasped at but not held,
it is the indiscernible.
These three qualities cannot be distinguished,
so consider them as one.

Above, there is no brightness.
Below, there is nothing concealed.
It is there but cannot be described
and returns again to nothingness.
It is a formless form,
a shape nonexistent.
It is the indistinct.

Meet it and do not find its beginnings.
Follow it and do not see its end.

Live by the ancient Tao to manage your current
affairs.
Understand our ancient origins.
This is the practice of Tao.

Notes: The Way of the cosmos (our ancient origins) cannot be defined; it is merely that which exists, that which is.

Living by the non-dualistic and impermanent nature of the cosmos, of which our existence is a part, frees one from the anxiety and discontent of striving to acquire or to become or to control. This is the practice of Tao— natural, spontaneous, fluid, and uncontrived.

第十五章

古之善為士者微妙玄通深不可識夫
唯不可識故強為之容豫兮若冬涉川
猶兮若畏四鄰儼兮其若客渙兮若冰
之將釋敦兮其若樸曠兮其若谷渾兮
其若濁孰能濁以靜之徐清孰能安以
久動之徐生保此道者不欲盈夫唯不
盈故能蔽不新

15

Stillness

The ancient masters had understanding so subtle,
so mysterious,
so profound and infinite,
it was wisdom beyond the known;
it was of the unknown.
As their insight was unknowable,
one can describe only their outward appearance:

> They were mindful,
> as if wading across a winter stream,
> alert and attentive to the uncertain world
> around them.
> Respectful and restrained,
> they were accepting,
> like melting ice.
> Gentle and unpretentious,
> they were open and free,
> like an untamed valley.

If water is muddy and unsettled,
what can still the turbidness until the water becomes
clear?
Can one possess an enduring tranquility until
action is necessary?

Embrace the Tao;
do not seek fulfillment.
Do not seek fulfillment,
and you will not know discontent.

Notes: A still mind, attentive and mindful, lives in harmony with the Tao.

第十六章

致虛極守靜篤萬物並作吾以觀復夫

物芸芸各復歸其根歸根曰靜是謂復

命復命曰常知常曰明不知常妄作凶

知常容容乃公公乃王王乃天天乃道

道乃久沒身不殆

16

A Still Mind Leads to Insight

Allow your mind to become utterly still
and observe the truth of the serene.
Earthly creatures and their activity,
I watch them flourish,
and then return to their beginnings.
Man and animal, all,
return once again to their roots.
Returning to one's roots is to become still;
that is, to rediscover what is life.
To rediscover life is to clearly understand.
Without clear understanding,
one acts impulsively and destructively.
With understanding,
one is tolerant and accepting,
thus just and honorable.
Just and honorable,
thus noble.
Noble,
thus of the Heavens.
Of the Heavens,
thus of the Tao.
Of the Tao,
thus eternal,
where even in death,
there is no peril.

Notes: A still mind free of egoism and arrogance and craving creates the mental conditions which lead to insight into the true nature of our interconnectedness with the external world and the uncontrived cycling of energy and matter as nature maintains its homeostatic balance. Thus, one can live in harmony with the Tao, freely and fearlessly and unfettered.

第十七章
大上下知有之其次親而譽之其次畏
之其次侮之信不足焉有不信焉悠兮
其貴言功成事遂百姓皆謂我自然

17

Leadership

The Greatest are merely known of.
The next are held Dear and Exalted.
Then there are the Feared.
And, finally,
the Disparaged.

Lack faith in the people,
and the people will have no faith in return.

There is little to pronounce;
simply accomplish what needs to be done,
and the people will say:

"We did it without effort."

Notes: A great leader inspires the people to act not through instilling fear, promoting dogma, or cultivating a cult of personality but by providing the materials and opportunities that allow the people to take care of themselves.

第十八章
大道廢有仁義智慧出有大偽六親不
和有孝慈國家昏亂有忠臣

18

Complementary Forces Arise

When the Tao has been abandoned,
benevolence and morality appear.

When wisdom and intelligence are commonplace,
deception and conspiracy emerge.

When family discord arises,
familial duty and paternal kindness come into
being.

When the country falls into chaos and upheaval,
virtuous and devoted patriots step forth.

*Notes: Regardless what conditions exist, complimentary forces arise as homeo-
stasis is naturally maintained. In the non-dualistic nature of Tao, there is no
better or worse but rather the regular cycling of one state to another, a constant
transformation and flux, trending toward wholeness and the absolute.*

第十九章
絕聖棄智民利百倍絕仁棄義民復孝
慈絕巧棄利盜賊無有此三者以為文
不足故令有所屬見素抱樸少私寡慾

19

Live Simply and Naturally

Reject the wise and holy men;
discard knowledge and wisdom,
and the benefit to the people
will be a hundredfold.

Reject goodness and morality,
and the people will respond
with respect and kindness.

Reject opportunism and profiteering,
and thieves and crooks
will be no more.

If these three propositions are insufficient, then:

Refer to the simple and the fundamental;
Do not be so self-absorbed;
Curb your desires.

Notes: It is not necessary to contrive dogmatic systems and principles to condition people's behavior.

Live spontaneously, with consideration for all, and do not be driven by unchecked cravings. This is the natural and healthful and harmonious way to live.

第二十章

絕學無憂唯之與阿相去幾何善之與
惡相去若何人之所畏不可不畏荒兮
其未央哉眾人熙熙如享太牢如春登
臺我獨泊兮其未兆如嬰兒之未孩儽
儽兮若無所歸眾人皆有餘而我獨若
遺我愚人之心也哉沌沌兮俗人昭昭
我獨昏昏俗人

20

Free and Non-striving

Renounce learning
and have no sorrows.
An "ah" is no more than several "eh"s.
Good and evil, as well,
are mutually related.
Must I fear what others fear?
Nonsense!

The masses appear to enjoy their busy lives
as if appreciating the terrace view on a spring day.

I, alone, fear the foreboding future,
much like an infant fears its future as a child.

Drifting,
it seems I have nowhere to which I can return.

All others have more than enough.
It is I alone who seems to have lost everything.

> What a fool I am!
> Chaos is coming!
>
> The common man is alert!
> I, alone, am in a stupor!

The people analyse meticulously;
I, alone, am indifferent.

The tranquility of the sea is endless.

All live their purposeful lives;

I, alone, resemble the stupid and vulgar.
Unlike the others,
I value being nourished by the Source of creation.

Notes: Does the society we have been raised in not condition us to follow cultural modes of particular behaviors, values, principles, beliefs, and so on? Who is to objectively determine what is correct or incorrect, what is good and what is bad?

To the dualistic-minded, following the traditions and habits and mores of that to which we have been conditioned is the "right" way to live; otherwise, we are the fearful, the anxious, the unmotivated, the directionless, the useless, the foolish, the stuporous, the stupid, the vulgar. To the non-dualistic minded, "correct" and "incorrect" are purely mental constructs. The life of one who is in harmony with the Tao lives actively and freely and spontaneously, without striving—wú wéi—like an infant who fears its future as a child, that is, not at all; like the sea, which is tranquil and endless and in tune with the rhythms of nature, the Tao, the Source of creation.

第二十一章

孔德之容惟道是從道之為物惟恍惟

惚惚兮恍兮其中有象恍兮惚兮其中

有物窈兮冥兮其中有精其精甚真其

中有信自今及古其名不去以閱眾甫

吾何以知眾甫之狀哉以此

21

Existence of Tao

The only way of the Virtuous
is the way of Tao.

Elusive and indistinct,
indistinct and elusive,
it appears.

Elusive and indistinct,
it has form.

Obscure and dark,
it contains the essence,
and within the essence,
there is absolute reality and truth.

From the beginning until now,
its existence has always been.

Thus, I know.
And how do I know?
By this way, do I know.

Notes: The Tao is and has always been; it is the action of living in harmony with all, the "ten thousand things under the heavens" as one whole, a singular life essence. One cannot see the "Tao" or define the "Tao" as a particular thing, yet it exists around you, right now. It is the happening, the occurring, the movement and interconnectedness of energy and matter swirling through and around you, at this very moment, and at every moment.

第二十二章

曲則全枉則直窪則盈敝則新少則得
多則惑是以聖人抱一為天下式不自
見故明不自是故彰不自伐故有功不
自矜故長夫唯不爭故天下莫能與之
爭古之所謂曲則全者豈虛言哉誠全
而歸之

22

Interconnectedness and Balance—Naturalness

Wrongs will be corrected.
The crooked will be straightened.
The empty will be filled.
The destroyed will be renewed.
The deficient will acquire.
The more one has,
the greater will be the confusion.

The Sage embraces a particular way for this earthly existence:

> Not self-obsessed,
> therefore clear-sighted;
>
> Not boastful,
> therefore recognized;
>
> Not arrogant,
> therefore appreciated by others;
>
> Not conceited,
> therefore never forgotten.
>
> Do not contend with others,
> and you cannot be contended with.

Is it not true, as the ancients say, that "wrongs will be corrected"?
Indeed, righteousness returns,
and wholeness is restored.

第二十三章

希言自然故飄風不終朝驟雨不終日

孰為此者天地天地尚不能久而況於

人乎故從事於道者同於道德者同於

德失者同於失同於道者道亦樂得之

同於德者德亦樂得之同於失者失亦

樂得之信不足焉有不信焉

23

Be One with What Is

To speak few words is natural.
An irregular gust of wind does not last all morning.
A sudden cloudburst does not last all day.
Who is the creator of these things?

Heaven and Earth!

Heaven and Earth are at one with impermanent conditions.

And what of man?

Those who follow the Tao
are at one with the way of the Tao.

Those who are Virtuous
are at one with the way of Virtue.

Those who have no identity
are at one with the way of the Egoless.

When at one with the way of the Tao,
the Tao is joyfully accepted.

When at one with the way of Virtue,
Virtue is cheerfully realized.

When at one with the way of the Egoless,
the way of the Egoless is happily received.

When belief is insufficient,
there is no belief.

第二十四章

企者不立跨者不行自見者不明自是者不彰自伐者無功自矜者不長其在道也曰餘食贅行物或惡之故有道者不處

24

Moderation and Balance

One standing on tiptoe
cannot stand firm.

One taking elongated strides
is not walking.

The self-obsessed
cannot see clearly
anything else.

> The boastful are ignored.
> The arrogant benefit none.
> The conceited are soon forgotten.

In the way of Tao,
these things are indulgent excesses,
like uneaten food wasted after a meal,
or superfluous behavior,
crudeness not found in the house of one who
follows the Tao.

第二十五章

有物混成先天地生寂兮寥兮獨立而不改周行而不殆可以為天下母吾不知其名字之曰道強為之名曰大大曰逝逝曰遠遠曰反故道強為大天大地大王亦大域中有四大而王居其一焉人法地地法天天法道道法自然

25

The Nature of Tao

From the primordial slime,
the innate arises into being.

> Silent.

> Empty.

> Solitary.

> Unchanging.

> Circulating.

> Tranquil.

> Becoming the source of all under
> the Heavens.

I do not know its name;
say it is Tao.

If I must, I call it "the transcendent."
To transcend means to die.
To die means to be removed from.
To be removed from means to transform.

The ancient Tao is transcendent.
Heaven is transcendent.
The Earth is transcendent.
The leader of men can also be transcendent.

Within our domain are the four forces,

of which the leader of men is one.

The way of man is the way of Earth.

The way of Earth is the way of Heaven.

The way of Heaven is the way of Tao.

The way of Tao is Naturalness.

第二十六章

重為輕根靜為躁君是以聖人終日行

不離輜重雖有榮觀燕處超然奈何萬

乘之主而以身輕天下輕則失本躁則

失君

26

Remain Mindful and Unperturbed

Heaviness serves as the root for lightness.

Stillness is the master of agitation.

The Sage,
traveling throughout the day,
never strays from vital essentials.
Although the scenery is magnificent,
the Sage is untouched,
remaining quietly in repose.
What a pity, then,
that the Lord of 10,000 Chariots
treats his rule with such reckless disregard.

Regard too lightly
and you will lose the root,
your essential foundation.

Rule with agitation and impatience
and you will lose your authority.

第二十七章

善行無轍跡善言無瑕讁善數不用籌策善閉無關楗而不可開善結無繩約而不可解是以聖人常善救人故無棄人常善救物故無棄物是謂襲明故善人者不善人之師不善人者善人之資不貴其師不愛其資雖智大迷是謂要妙

27

Virtue with Humility

Honorable actions leave no trace.
Just and honest speech has no fault to be criticized.
One proficient at counting does not need markers.

A door that closes well needs no lock,
and still, it cannot be opened.

Something secured well needs no rope to bind it,
yet, it does not come loose.

Thus, the Sage is benevolent to all
and abandons no one.
The Sage cares for all creatures
and neglects not one.
This is called
"Acquisition of Understanding".

Hence, the compassionate are teachers for the
unpleasant;
the unpleasant are a source of concern for the
compassionate.
Regardless of how knowledgeable one might be, a
person who does not value his or her teachers or
one who does not value that which provides him
or her purpose lacks insight.

This is an essential insight.

Notes: Virtuous and honest action has no intention. It is simply a manifestation of insight into the nature of Tao.

第二十八章

知其雄守其雌為天下谿為天下谿常
德不離復歸於嬰兒知其白守其黑為
天下式為天下式常德不忒復歸於無
極知其榮守其辱為天下谷常德乃足
復歸於樸樸散則為器聖人用之則為
官長故大制不割

28

Remain Constant and Resolute

Know what is strength
and remain humble.

Be the river flowing beneath the heavens,
which is to be Virtuous and constant,
returning as a newborn (full of infinite potential).

Know the light and observe the darkness.

Be the archetype for earthly existence.

As the archetype,
stay honourable and resolute,
returning again to the Infinite.

Know what is honor and guard against disgrace,
becoming a Valley of this heavenly creation.

And when Eternal Virtue is restored,
revert to the plain and simple.

Dispense plainness and simplicity as tools,
the Sage does,
hence government officials endure
and institutions do not crumble.

Notes: Remain constant and resolute, humbly returning to the Tao; then, all will endure.

第二十九章

將欲取天下而為之吾見其不得已天下神器不可為也為者敗之執者失之故物或行或隨或歔或吹或強或羸或挫或隳是以聖人去甚去奢去泰

29

Reject the Extreme

The desire to possess
all beneath the heavens,
I see it cannot be resisted.

The universe is sacred
and cannot be appropriated.

Appropriated,
it will be destroyed.

Possessed,
it will be lost.

Hence, earthly entities sometimes lead
and sometimes follow,
sometimes inhale sharply
and sometimes exhale lightly;
are sometimes dominant
and sometimes dominated;
sometimes bend
and sometimes break.

The Sage, therefore,
rejects the extreme,
rejects the extravagant,
rejects the grandiose.

*Notes: Actions taken to their extremes lead to disharmony and imbalance.
Maintain the center. Avoid the conflict of complementary forces arising to
their greatest intensity as the Constant, the Tao, trends toward a homeostatic
state of wholeness.*

第三十章

以道佐人主者不以兵強天下其事好
遠師之所處荊棘生焉大軍之後必有
凶年善者果而已不以取強果而勿矜
果而勿伐果而勿驕果而不得已果而
勿強物壯則老是謂不道不道早已

30

Non-violence—Act without Egoistic Intent

Assisting the leader of men by the way of Tao,
do not advise using military power to rule;
this approach is best rejected.
For wherever armies are dispatched,
thorny brambles are born in the fields.
And when the armies have gone,
there is certain to be a year of famine.

The Virtuous are resolute,
nothing more,
by no means acquire by force.

> Achieve results without glorifying.
> Achieve results without boasting.
> Achieve results without pridefulness.
> Achieve results because it happens of its own accord.
> Achieve results without intention.

Once something's power robustly peaks,
its strength then declines.
This is not the way of Tao.

Neglect to follow the Tao
and come to an early end.

第三十一章

夫佳兵者不祥之器物或惡之故有道者不處君子居則貴左用兵則貴右兵者不祥之器非君子之器不得已而用之恬淡為上勝而不美而美之者是樂殺人夫樂殺人者則不可以得志於天下矣吉事尚左凶事尚右偏將軍居左上將軍居右

31

Victory in War

Fine weapons and soldiers are tools of menace,
signs of impending brutality,
loathed by all.
Thus, followers of the Tao are not associated with
these instruments of violence.

The Honorable follow the left (and are concerned
with safeguarding and preservation).
Barbarians follow the right (and are warlike and
thuggish).

Weapons and war
are never the desire of the Noble,
but when their necessity is unavoidable,
they are used without glory or pride.
Thus, victory brings no glory,
because only the vainglorious take pleasure in
killing.
And one who takes pleasure in killing
can never be champion of the people.

Prosperity and fortune symbolize the left,
foreboding and deprivation the right.
Second-in-command on the left,
and head-of-command on the right,
when they speak of war,
they should speak as if conducting a funeral.

Slaughter of the many
is a reason to weep with grief.

Victory in war is celebrated
by mourning the dead.

第三十二章

道常無名樸雖小天下莫能臣也侯王

若能守之萬物將自賓天地相合以降

甘露民莫之令而自均始制有名名亦

既有夫亦將知止知止所以不殆譬道

之在天下猶川穀之於江海

32

Constant and Unperturbed

The Tao is nameless and plain, tiny,
but subservient to none.

When noblemen and emperors abide by the Tao,
all will come forth to honor it.
Heaven and Earth will become one,
and the life-giving raindrops will fall.

The people do not have control over their lives, so
systems are established and given names.
When a name exists,
limits are defined,
and knowing limitations
is how one feels secure.

The Tao of the Heavens is like a valley river
that flows constant into the sea.

Notes: We create names and systems, trying to exert control over our lives in an effort to alleviate fear and uncertainty. It is unnecessary, and futile. The Tao is flowing and constant, spontaneous and natural. There is no need for uncertainty or fear, no need to cling to traditions and words. Follow the Tao and things will occur when they need to occur.

第三十三章
知人者智自知者明勝人者有力自勝
者強知足者富強行者有志不失其所
者久死而不亡者壽

33

Insight and the Eternal

One who understands others is wise;
one who understands one's self is enlightened.

One with mastery over others displays power;
one with mastery over one's self displays strength.

One who knows contentment is rich.

One who is determined has purpose.

One who knows where he or she belongs endures.

One who dies but does not cease (to inspire)
is eternal.

第三十四章

大道氾兮其可左右萬物恃之而生

而不辭功成不名有衣養萬物而不

為主常無欲可名於小萬物歸焉而

不為主可名為大以其終不自為大

故能成其大

34

The Tao—Ordinary and Accessible

The Tao flows through all.
To the left, to the right,
it is everywhere.
All life relies on it,
grows from it,
and it refuses none.
When the work is complete,
it is not recognized.

All earthly creatures are provided for,
yet they are not ruled over.

Without desire or intention,
it can be called lowly and small.

All living things return to it,
yet it is not their ruler.

It may be called magnificent,
but it does not claim magnificence.
Hence, it is truly magnificent.

第三十五章

執大象天下往往而不害安平太樂與

餌過客止道之出口淡乎其無味視之

不足見聽之不足聞用之不足既

35

The Tao Needs No Followers, and Endures

Display a great image,
and all are attracted to you.

Seek out security,
and live too passively.

Where music and good food are found,
travelers end their journey.

The Tao departs.

Weak and tasteless,
it is looked at but not seen.
Heard but not distinguished,
it is used but never exhausted.

Notes: The Tao seeks nothing in particular, and endures quietly, without striving.

第三十六章

將欲歙之必固張之將欲弱之必固強

將欲廢之必固興之將欲奪之必固

之將欲微明柔弱勝剛強魚不可脫

與之是謂微明柔弱勝剛強魚不可脫

於淵國之利器不可以示人

36

The Subtle Insight

The impetus to shrink arises, certainly,
from that which has expanded.

The impetus to become weak arises, certainly, from
that which has been strong.

The impetus to be abolished arises, certainly,
from that which has been established.

The impetus to be forcibly seized arises, certainly,
from that which has been provided.

This is called the Subtle Insight:

> The soft and weak overcome the solid and
> strong.
> Just as fish should not rise from their deep
> pools,
> a country's strengths should not be displayed
> for all to see.

*Notes: Every state of being has its complementary state, which spontaneously
and naturally arises when the symbiotic relationship becomes unbalanced.*

*To endure, it is best for a country, or anyone for that matter, to remain
humble, reserved, and unassuming.*

第三十七章

道常無為而無不為侯王若能守之萬
物將自化化而欲作吾將鎮之以無名
之樸無名之樸夫亦將無欲不欲以靜
天下將自定

37

A Still Mind Recognizes Truth

The Tao does not strive,
yet all is cared for.

If officials and emperors could abide by the Tao,
all earthly creatures would flourish naturally.
And if they yearn still for more,
I would restrain their desires with the plain and simple,
with that which cannot be named,
this unnamed for which I also have no desire.

Freedom from desire is stillness of mind,
where I realize that all under the heavens
are in their place.

Notes: A still mind experiences the truth of non-striving—wú wéi.

第三十八章

上德不德是以有德下德不失德是以無德上德無為而無以為下德為之而有以為上仁為之而無以為上義為之而有以為上禮為之而莫之應則攘臂而扔之故失道而後德失德而後仁而後義失義而後禮夫禮者忠信之薄而亂之首

38

"Virtue" vs. "virtue"

A person of Virtue has no desire to be virtuous;
thus, there is Virtue.

A person of inferior Virtue does not know the
absence of virtue; thus, there is no Virtue.

The Virtuous do not act with intention; therefore,
there is no recognition.

The less Virtuous contrive their actions; thus,
there is acknowledgment.

The compassionate act without motivation.

The righteous act when there is motivation.

When the dogmatic act and none respond,
those who are non-responsive are rejected.

Hence, when the Tao is lost,
virtue appears.
When virtue is lost,
compassion appears.
When compassion is lost,
righteousness appears.
When righteousness is lost,
dogma appears.

The feebleness of the dogmatic is
faith and loyalty,
the beginnings of confusion.

Previous scholars claim the Tao as magnificent; this
is the commencement of stupidity.

Those of character dwell in the meaningful,
not the superficial;
live in reality,
not in superlatives.

Therefore, reject the other
and accept this.

Notes: There is: **Virtue**, *and there is:* **virtue***.*

Virtue: *If Tao is truth about the nature of our existence, Virtue is the
action that arises from recognition of these truths. When one's actions manifest themselves from the truths of non-duality, impermanence, non-striving,
and naturalness, this is a life lived with Virtue, with no desire to be or to
become anything, virtuous or otherwise.*

virtue (noun): *a quality or practice contrived upon some dualistic notion
of moral excellence or righteousness.*

第三十九章

昔之得一者天得一以清地得一以寧神得一以靈谷得一以盈萬物得一以生侯王得一以為天下貞其致之天無以清將恐裂地無以寧將恐發神無以靈將恐歇谷無以盈將恐竭萬物無以生將恐滅侯王無以貴高將恐蹶故貴以賤為本高

39

Wholeness Leads to Unity and Harmony

In those times when Oneness was realized,
the Sky, unified and whole,
became clear and pure.

The Earth, unified and whole,
became stable and peaceful.

The Spirits, unified and whole,
became alert and productive.

The Valley, unified and whole,
filled to abundance.

Earthly Creatures, unified and whole,
all flourished.

Noblemen and Emperors, unified and whole,
knowing all under the Heavens to be pure and
undefiled, were devoted to its wellbeing.

If the Sky is not clear and pure,
be fearful that it will split apart.

If the Earth is not stable and peaceful,
be fearful that it will burst into chaos.

If the Spirits are not alert and productive,
be fearful that they will impotently wither away.

If the Valley is not filled to abundance,
be fearful that it will be depleted.

If the Earthly Creatures do not flourish,
be fearful that they will go extinct.

If Noblemen and Emperors are not respected,
be fearful that they will be subverted.

Thus, the humble masses are the foundation of the aristocrats.

The high is based on the low.

The nobility, therefore, refer to themselves as the "lone," the "few," the "destitute".

Is it not the humble masses upon which all is dependent?

To have others frequently convey praise
is no longer praise at all.

Do not desire a jade necklace any more than
if it were made of stone.

第四十章
反者道之動弱者道之用天下萬物生
於有有生於無

40

Tao Principles

To return is the action of the Tao.

To yield is the application of the Tao.

All earthly creatures under the heavens are born into existence.

Existence is born from non-existence.

第四十一章

上士聞道勤而行之中士聞道若存若
亡下士聞道大笑之不笑不足以為道
故建言有之明道若昧進道若退夷道
若纇上德若谷大白若辱廣德若不足
建德若偷質真若渝大方無隅大器晚
成大音希聲大象無形道隱無名夫唯
道善貸且成

41

Understanding the Tao

The insightful, having learned of the Tao,
embrace it as a way of life.

The average, having learned of the Tao,
study it, and then forget it.

The ignorant, having learned of the Tao,
burst out in laughter.

If it were not laughed at,
it would not be the Tao.

Therefore, it is said:

> The Path to clarity seems like obscurity.
> The Path to progress seems like regression.
> The smoothest Path seems uneven.
>
> The highest Virtue seems coarse.
> The greatest purity seems besmirched.
> Abundant Virtue seems inadequate.
> The establishment of Virtue seems devious.
>
> Genuine character seems treacherous.
>
> An expansive area has no corners.
>
> Great things take time to accomplish.
>
> Exquisite musical notes are rare tones.
>
> A large shape has no form.

The Tao, unseen,
is beyond description.

The Tao, alone,
nourishes Virtue,
bringing all to fulfillment.

*Notes: The Tao is not realized by studying concepts or acquiring knowledge.
The Tao is realized by recognizing the truth, and then living it: non-duality,
impermanence, non-striving, naturalness and an interconnectedness to nature.*

第四十二章

道生一一生二二生三三生萬物萬物

負陰而抱陽沖氣以為和人之所惡唯

孤寡不穀而王公以為稱故物或損之

而益或益之而損人之所教我亦教之

強梁者不得其死吾將以為教父

42

Creation and Death

The Tao gave birth to One (the Whole, the
Absolute).
The One gave birth to Two (yin and yang).
The Two gave birth to Three (Heaven, Earth, and
Dé [Virtue]).
And the Three gave birth to all living things.

All living things carry yin and embrace yang.
By combining these energies,
they achieve harmony.

These things we abhor:

> To be lonely;
> To be partnerless;
> To be impoverished.

Princes and nobles also consider this so.

Hence, one might benefit from a loss
and suffer from a benefit.

What others have taught, I also teach:

> The powerful and well-established
> cannot accept their death.

This I consider the author of my teaching.

Notes: Do no cling to dualities and there is no fear of death.

第四十三章
天下之至柔馳騁天下之至堅無有入
無閒吾是以知無為之有益不言之教
無為之益天下希及之

43

Emptiness and Non-striving

The softest, most yielding
overcomes the solid and most unyielding.

That which has no form or substance
can still enter a space that is filled.

Thus, I know the value of non-striving.

Teach without words.

Gain by not striving.

Few can truly understand.

第四十四章
名與身孰親身與貨孰多得與亡孰病
是故甚愛必大費多藏必厚亡知足不
辱知止不殆可以長久

44

Live Long and Endure

Which is more treasured,
fame or health?

Which is more valued,
health or possessions?

Which causes more suffering,
gain or loss?

Those things that you covet, then,
come with great cost.

Amassing great treasures
entails profound loss.

Know contentment,
and there is no self-doubt.

Know when to stop,
and there is no danger.

In this way, one can live long and endure.

第四十五章

大成若缺其用不弊大盈若沖其用不

窮大直若屈大巧若拙大辯若訥躁勝

寒靜勝熱清靜為天下正

45

Peace and Tranquility

A great accomplishment may seem imperfect,
yet its usefulness endures.

Great satisfaction may seem uninspired,
yet it is inexhaustible.

The straightest seem crooked.

The most skilled seem clumsy.

The most eloquent seem cautious.

Calmness overcomes impatience.

Coolness overcomes heat.

Peace and tranquility result in all beneath the
heavens coming to order.

Notes: A peaceful mind, tranquil and unstriving, finds all as it should be.

第四十六章
天下有道卻走馬以糞天下無道戎馬
生於郊禍莫大於不知足咎莫大於欲
得故知足之足常足矣

46

Contentment is Tranquility

When the Tao is present,
horses are ridden to care for the fields.

When the Tao is absent,
warhorses appear on the outskirts.

The greatest affliction is having a constant desire
for more.

The greatest curse is the lack of contentment.

The greatest torment: the want to possess.

Therefore, know what is contentment
and always have enough.

第四十七章
不出戶知天下不闚牖見天道其出彌
遠其知彌少是以聖人不行而知不見
而名不為而成

47

Seeking Truth not Knowledge

Without leaving one's house,
one can understand all earthly things.

Without looking through a window,
one can see the ways of Heaven.

The further one goes out seeking,
the less one knows.

Thus, the Sage knows without seeking,
sees clearly without looking,
and succeeds without intention.

Notes: This Chapter refers to Chapter One, i.e., "To acquire knowledge is to create mental constructs. The Tao, the truth, is not a concept but rather what is: the existence of energy and material forms and their interrelationships in the external world."

The search for knowledge is the desire for an accumulation of mental constructs. The truth is present before you. The truth is what is.

第四十八章

為學日益為道日損損之又損以至於
無為無為而無不為取天下常以無事
及其有事不足以取天下

48

Lessening Knowledge

In order to gain knowledge,
one adds and accumulates,
day after day.

In order to practice the Tao,
one subtracts and reduces,
day by day;
becoming less and less,
until there is no more striving.

In non-striving,
nothing is left undone.

The way to govern the earthly realm
is to never have the intention to act upon it.
For when the intention to act emerges,
the world cannot be governed.

第四十九章
聖人無常心以百姓心為心善者吾善
之不善者吾亦善之德善信者吾信之
不信者吾亦信之德信聖人在天下歙
歙焉為天下渾其心百姓皆注其耳目
聖人皆孩之

49

Non-discrimination and Virtue

The Sage has not his or her own mind
but regards the needs and feelings of the people as
his or her own.

> To the kind,
> I am kind.
>
> To the unkind,
> I am also kind,
> because Virtue is kindness.
>
> To the faithful,
> I am faithful.
>
> To the unfaithful,
> I am also faithful,
> because Virtue is faithfulness.

Dwelling in the earthly realm,
the Sage maintains for the world
a heart that does not discriminate.

While the common people discriminate with their
eyes and ears,
the Sage treats all as his or her own children.

第五十章

出生入死生之徒十有三死之徒十有
三人之生動之死地亦十有三夫何故
以其生生之厚蓋聞善攝生者陸行不
遇兕虎入軍不被甲兵兕無所投其角
虎無所措其爪兵無所容其刃夫何故
以其無死地

50

Fearlessness

When we are born,
we enter the sphere of death.

> Three of ten live with vitality.
>
> Three of ten live with a concern for death.
>
> And three of ten are born,
> occupy their lives with activity,
> and then die.

Why is this so?

Each way follows the significance with which a
person characterizes his or her life.

> The One who disregards renown and promi-
> nence, living for the good, travels the land and
> does not encounter bulls or tigers. When
> entering battle, he or she is not touched by the
> weapons of war. The bull can find no place to
> gore; the tiger, no place to claw; weapons of
> war, nowhere to pierce.

Why is this so?

Because for this One,
there is no realm of death.

*Notes: To live by the Tao is to recognize death and to live a life of Virtue,
which means to live without fear.*

第五十一章

道生之德畜之物形之勢成之是以萬
物莫不尊道而貴德道之尊德之貴夫
莫之命而常自然故道生之德畜之長
之育之亭之毒之養之覆之生
為而不恃長而不宰是謂玄德

51

Tao and Virtue

All things are born from Tao,
and all are nourished by Virtue.

Formed from matter
and shaped by conditions,
all earthly creatures,
without exception,
defer to the Tao and esteem Virtue.

Deferring to the Tao and esteeming Virtue
are of the natural order.

The Tao and Virtue are commanded by none.

Hence, all things are born of the Tao.
All things are nourished by Virtue.

> Fostering and nurturing,
>
> sheltering from harm,
>
> supporting and protecting,
>
> giving birth but not possessing,
>
> serving but not creating dependence,
>
> cultivating but not governing,
>
> this is called the Mystical Virtue.

第五十二章

天下有始以為天下母既得其母以知
其子既知其子復守其母沒身不殆塞
其兌閉其門終身不勤開其兌濟其事
其兌閉其門終身不勤開其兌濟其事光
終身不救見小曰明守柔曰強用其光
復歸其明無遺身殃是為習常

52

Nature and the Eternal

There was the beginning of earthly existence, which
we can call the mother of all living creatures.
Recognize the mother and understand her children
(all living creatures).
Know that when children return to abide by their
mother, there exists no mortal peril.

Block the passageways (of the mind, i.e., listening
and speaking, accumulating and expounding on
ideas),
shut the doors (of intent),
and one's life is effortless.

Stimulate the passageways (of the mind),
strive to accomplish,
and live in futility.

To see the subtle is to have Insight.

To remain yielding against force is to be strong.

Use the brightness (of insight) to return to mental
clarity,
and your life will know no tragedy.

This is practicing the Eternal.

*Notes: What is the eternal but that which never changes. And what never
changes but truth.*

*Return to the Tao and practice the Eternal by recognizing these truths:
non-duality, impermanence, naturalness, and an interconnectedness to nature.*

第五十三章

使我介然有知行於大道唯施是畏大
道甚夷而民好徑朝甚除田甚蕪倉甚
虛服文綵帶利劍厭飲食財貨有餘是
為盜誇非道也哉

53

Losing the Way

Making my mind aware
and traveling by the Tao,
the only thing I must deal with is fear.

The Tao, though, is utterly safe,
when one attentively follows the Path.

When Insight is lost,
fields are choked with weeds
and granaries become bare.

Meanwhile, beautiful clothing and cultural
activities flourish,
lethal weapons are carried openly,
necessities of food and drink are ignored
as excessive wealth become displays of which the
plunderers and capitalists may boast.

This is certainly not the way of Tao!

第五十四章

善建者不拔善抱者不脫子孫以祭祀不輟修之於身其德乃真修之於家其德乃餘修之於鄉其德乃長修之於國其德乃豐修之於天下其德乃普故以身觀身以家觀家以鄉觀鄉以國觀國以天下觀天下吾何以知天下然哉以此

54

Cultivate Virtue, Cultivate Harmony

That which is well-established
is not easily uprooted.

That which is truly cherished
is not easily lost.

From generation to generation,
all will be forever grateful to their forebears.

> Cultivate Virtue in yourself,
> and Virtue will become reality.
>
> Cultivate Virtue in a family,
> and Virtue will be plentiful.
>
> Cultivate Virtue in a village,
> and Virtue will develop.
>
> Cultivate Virtue in a nation,
> and Virtue will be abundant.
>
> Cultivate Virtue under all the heavens,
> and Virtue will be universal.

Thus, one keeps watch over oneself.
A family keeps watch over the family.
A village keeps watch over the village.
A nation keeps watch over the nation.
The Heavens keep watch over the Heavens.

How do I know this is so?
By my keeping watch!

Notes: When one's actions manifest themselves from the truths of non-duality, impermanence, non-striving, and naturalness, a life of Virtue is lived. Live a life of Virtue and harmony will be realized.

第五十五章

含德之厚比於赤子蜂蠆虺蛇不螫猛獸不據攫鳥不搏骨弱筋柔而握固未知牝牡之合而全作精之至也終日號而不嗄和之至也知和曰常知常曰明益生曰祥心使氣曰強物壯則老謂之不道不道早已

55

The Heart of a Child

One who is rich in Virtue
is like a newborn infant.

> Bees and scorpions will not sting.
> Predators will not attack.
> Bones are soft and muscles are supple,
> yet this person's grip is powerful.
> The union of female and male might be
> unknown,
> still, this individual is not at all limited.
> Infused with vitality and vigor,
> he or she can roar out all day without
> becoming hoarse;
> this is absolute harmony.

To understand harmony is to be steadfast.
To understand being steadfast is to have a clear
mind.
To nurture one's life is to promote good fortune.
To be mindful of the breath is to be strong and
powerful.
To robustly exert oneself is to soon wither,
which is not of the Tao.

That which is contrary to the Tao
does not endure.

*Notes: To live according to Tao is to approach life with the heart of a child,
i.e., to experience the natural world and the action of living with: wonder,
curiosity, amazement, spontaneity, fearlessness, and joy, and without: expectation, attainment, connivance, and fear.*

第五十六章

知者不言言者不知塞其兌閉其門挫

其銳解其分和其光同其塵是謂玄同

故不可得而親不可得而疏不可得而

利不可得而害不可得而貴不可得而

賤故為天下貴

56

Freedom

One who knows
does not speak.

One who speaks
does not know.

Block the passageways (of the mind, i.e., listening
and speaking, accumulating and expounding on
ideas).
Shut the doors (of intent).
Blunt the sharpness (of emotion).
Dissolve uncertainties into clarity.
Become one with the dust of the earth.
This is called the Profound Oneness.
And in this state,

> One cannot be loved nor rejected;
> Cannot be benefited nor harmed;
> Cannot be celebrated nor denounced.

This, under the heavens,
is the rarest state of being.

Notes: One who lives in harmony with the Tao is non-dualistic and non-striving, thus, can live with spontaneity, naturalness, and non-egoistic fearlessness.

第五十七章

以正治國以奇用兵以無事取天下吾
何以知其然哉以此天下多忌諱而民
彌貧民多利器國家滋昏人多伎巧奇
物滋起法令滋彰盜賊多有故聖人云
我無為而民自化我好靜而民自正我
無事而民自富我無欲而民自樸

57

Self-government

Rule a nation with fairness and integrity.

Conduct military operations with unpredictability.

Lead all under the heavens without striving for anything.

How can I know this is so?
I know by this:

> When more social taboos and ritual
> prohibitions exist,
> people become incompetent.

> When the people have more lethal weapons,
> the nation becomes increasingly chaotic.

> When people are more skillful and clever,
> more oddities arise in society.

> When laws and regulations increase,
> more thieves and robbers appear.

Therefore, the Sage says:

> I do not strive for anything,
> and the people themselves will transform.

> I stay calm and still,
> and the people themselves will become just.

I have no affairs to attend to,
and the people themselves will prosper.

I have no desire,
and the people themselves will live simply.

Notes: As long as people recognize the truth of Tao and live with Virtue, there is no need for authoritarian governance. When the people live by the truths of: non-duality, impermanence, spontaneity, naturalness and interconnectedness, they will live naturally and spontaneously in harmony with nature and one another.

第五十八章

其政悶悶其民淳淳其政察察其民缺

缺禍兮福之所倚福兮禍之所伏孰知

其極其無正正復為奇善復為妖人之

迷其日固久是以聖人方而不割廉而

不劌直而不肆光而不燿

58

The Way of the Sage

When a government has no ambition,
its people will be sincere and honest.

When a government is invasive and scrutinizing,
its people will become unethical and deceitful.

Disaster complements good fortune.
Good fortune complements disaster.

Who knows what will happen?

The normal revert to being the unusual.
The benevolent revert to being the fiendish.
Man's confusion will endure for an extended time.

> Thus, the Sage is sharp
> but not cutting;
>
> is honest
> but not hurtful;
>
> is frank
> but not belligerent;
>
> is bright
> but not dazzling.

第五十九章

治人事天莫若嗇夫唯嗇是謂早服早
服謂之重積德重積德則無不克無不
克則莫知其極莫知其極可以有國有
國之母可以長久是謂深根固柢長生
久視之道

59

Governing a Nation

When managing the people's affairs
and caring for Nature,
one is not self-serving.

Not to be self-serving begins with
first abandoning one's ideas.

To abandon one's ideas
is to value Virtue,
without doubt.

To value Virtue without doubt
is to have no limits.

When one knows no limits,
one can found a nation.

And when a nation has a founder
who knows the Way of Nature,
the nation can endure,
which means there are deep roots
and a solid foundation.

A long life with a lasting vision is the Tao.

Notes: The "Heavens (天)" and later the "Mother (母)" refer to our origins, which have been translated as "Nature" and the "Way of Nature" respectively.

第六十章

治大國若烹小鮮以道蒞天下其鬼不神非其鬼不神其神不傷人非其神不傷人聖人亦不傷人夫兩不相傷故德交歸焉

60

Frying a Small Fish

Governing a great nation
is like frying a small fish.

Use the Tao to manage earthly matters,
and the demons and spirits will have no influence.

Not that the demons and spirits have no power
but that they will not do harm.

The demons and spirits will not do harm
and neither will the Sage do harm.

That is, neither will harm the other.
Hence, the virtue of one complements the other.

Notes: At first glance, the first sentence appears rather nonsensical. What does "frying a small fish" have to do with governing a nation? Consider that the fire used to fry can destroy and do harm, but when it is applied constructively and in a mindful and moderate manner, fire can be of great benefit, i.e., use your power and authority constructively and mindfully.

The "demons and spirits" of the world may also seem to be things to avoid and fear, but follow the way of Tao and all will stay in its natural, balanced state of wholeness, the Absolute.

第六十一章

大國者下流天下之交天下之牝牝常
以靜勝牡以靜為下故大國以下小國
則取小國小國以下大國則取大國故
或下以取或下而取大國不過欲兼畜
人小國不過欲入事人夫兩者各得其
所欲大者宜為下

61

The Power of Humility

A great nation flows downward,
where all beneath the heavens intersect
and are of the feminine.

The feminine,
forever tranquil,
overcomes the masculine.
And the tranquility of the feminine
becomes its humble nature.

Thus, when a larger nation is humble towards a
smaller nation, it secures (the loyalty of) the smaller
nation.
When a smaller nation is humble towards a larger
nation, it secures (the benefits of) the larger nation.

One, therefore, secures what it wants
by having humility,
and the other secures what it wants
by maintaining humility.

A powerful nation hopes to nurture a greater
population.
A smaller nation hopes to participate in the affairs
of mankind.

By being humble and unpretentious,
both secure what they desire.

It is advisable, then,
for the powerful to practice humility.

第六十二章

道者萬物之奧善人之寶不善人之所
保美言可以市尊行可以加人人之不
善何棄之有故立天子置三公雖有拱
璧以先駟馬不如坐進此道古之所以
貴此道者何不曰以求得有罪以免邪
故為天下貴

62

Forgiveness

To all, the Tao is an ambiguity.
To the Virtuous, it is a treasure.
To the un-Virtuous, it is a shelter.

If beautiful words can be purchased
and honors can be contrived,
why should the un-Virtuous be abandoned?

Therefore, when the emperor is being established
and the three nobles appointed,
instead of presenting jade treasures and four
magnificent stallions,
it is better to curry no favor
and to offer the Tao.

Why did the ancients so value the Tao?
Because it allowed them to forgive those who had
done wrong.

Hence, the Tao is treasured by all.

第六十三章

為無為事無事味無味大小多少報怨以德圖難於其易為大於其細天下難事必作於易天下大事必作於細是以聖人終不為大故能成其大夫輕諾必寡信多易必多難是以聖人猶難之故終無難矣

63

Facing Difficulties

Take action without striving.

Do work without accomplishing.

> Taste the tasteless;
> enlarge the small;
> increase the few;
> repay bitterness with kindness.

Plan for the difficult
while it is still easy.

> Attend to greater things
> by taking care of the small.

All difficult matters must be dealt with
when they are easy.

> All great affairs must be done
> by taking care of the small affairs.

The Sage, therefore, makes no attempt to accomplish great things, and, thus, achieves greatness.

One who promises too readily
gains little trust.

One who lives with too little concern
will certainly have more problems.

Thus, the Sage, knowing that the difficult is not easily accomplished, has no difficulties.

第六十四章

其安易持，其未兆易謀，其脆易泮，其微易散，為之於未有，治之於未亂，合抱之木生於毫末，九層之臺起於累土，千里之行始於足下，為者敗之，執者失之，是以聖人無為故無敗，無執故無失，民之從事常於幾成而敗之，慎終如始則無敗事，是以聖

64

Action without Acting

If it is stable and secure,
it is easy to maintain.

> If there is no prediction,
> it is easy to plan.

If it is fragile,
it is easily destroyed.

> If it is small,
> it is easily lost.

Deal with matters
before troubles occur.

> Manage your affairs
> before things becomes chaotic.

A tree as great as one's embrace,
grows from a tiny seedling.

> A nine-story terrace
> arises from a mound of earth.

A thousand-mile journey
begins with the first step.

> One who acts with intention
> defeats oneself.

Things slip away
from one who grasps.

Thus, the Sage does not strive,
and in this way, does not fail.

The Sage does not grasp,
and hence, nothing slips away.

When people handle their affairs,
they often fail right at the moment of success.

Be as mindful in the end
as you are at the beginning;
then, there is no failure.

The Sage, therefore, seeks no desire;
treasures no precious objects;
learns to unlearn;
and returns people back to what they have neglected.

In this way, the Sage helps all living things naturally,
and dares not strive for anything.

第六十五章

古之善為道者非以明民將以愚之民

之難治以其智多故以智治國國之賊

不以智治國國之福知此兩者亦稽式

常知稽式是謂玄德玄德深矣遠矣與

物反矣然後乃至大順

65

Accumulating Knowledge

In ancient times, those who understood the Tao
made no effort to instruct others;
rather, they feigned ignorance.

When there is too much knowledge,
people are difficult to govern.

Thus, use knowledge to govern a country,
and the country is subverted.

Do not use knowledge to govern,
and the country experiences good fortune.

Be aware of these two alternatives
and respect this pattern.

To have constant awareness and consideration of
this pattern
is called the Mystical Virtue.

The Mystical Virtue, deep and remote, guides all
things back to accord with the Absolute.

第六十六章

江海所以能為百穀王者以其善下之故能為百穀王是以欲上民必以言下之欲先民必以身後之是以聖人處上而民不重處前而民不害是以天下樂推而不厭以其不爭故天下莫能與之爭

66

Lead with Humility

Why can the rivers and seas lord over the hundred valleys?
It is because the rivers and seas lie at a lower level;
this allows them to rule the valleys.

Thus, to govern the people,
one must be humble in speech.

To lead the people,
one must follow.

Hence, when the Sage administers to the people,
the people will not be a burden.

When the Sage appears before the people,
the people will do the Sage no harm.

Then, all beneath the heavens will advocate joy,
not animosity,
and there will be no conflict.

All beneath the heavens will live without struggle
or discord.

第六十七章

天下皆謂我道大似不肖夫唯大故似不肖若肖久矣其細也夫我有三寶持而保之一曰慈二曰儉三曰不敢為天下先故慈故能勇儉故能廣不敢為天先故能成器長今舍慈且勇舍儉且廣舍後且先死矣夫慈以戰則勝以守則固天將救之

67

Three Treasures

All under the heavens say my Tao is so profound
that it seems like nonsense.

Because it is most profound,
of course it seems like nonsense.

If it were not like nonsense,
it would have become insignificant long ago.

I have three treasures that I maintain and preserve:

> The first is compassion;
> The second is moderating oneself;
> And the third is that I dare not put myself
> before anything else under the heavens.

Having compassion
allows one to be courageous.

Moderating oneself
allows one to be generous.

Maintaining humility
allows one to be a good leader.

In these times,
people have abandoned compassion
and have distanced themselves from courage;

People do not believe in moderation
and have distanced themselves from generosity;

People have forgotten humility
and have distanced themselves from being leaders.

All are doomed.

Be compassionate in battle
and find victory.

To protect others
be resolute.

The Heavens will look out for those
who are compassionate and protective.

第六十八章
善為士者不武善戰者不怒善勝敵者
不與善用人者為之下是謂不爭之德
是謂用人之力是謂配天古之極

68

Action without Conflict

A good soldier
is not violent.

A good fighter
is not angry.

A victorious competitor
does not antagonize.

One who most effectively employs others
is humble.

This is:

> The Virtue of not competing and the Power
> of employing others.

This is called:

> Becoming one with nature
> at its most primal and basic.

第六十九章

用兵有言吾不敢為主而為客不敢進

寸而退尺是謂行無行攘無臂扔無敵

執無兵禍莫大於輕敵輕敵幾喪吾寶

故抗兵相加哀者勝矣

69

War

There is a saying among military strategists:

> When one dares not play the host,
> play the guest.

> When one dares not advance an inch,
> retreat a foot.

> This is called moving without motion;
> resisting without rising up;
> opposing without opposition;
> executing a plan without attacking.

There is no greater disaster
than underestimating an enemy.

Underestimating an enemy is like
arranging a funeral for all that one treasures.

When mutually opposing forces go to war,
those who can grieve the most will be victorious.

第七十章

吾言甚易知甚易行天下莫能知莫能

行言有宗事有君夫唯無知是以不我

知知我者希則我者貴是以聖人被褐

懷玉

70

The Uncommon Sage

What I say is easy to understand and to practice.

Yet, there are few under the heavens
who can understand it or practice it.

The words I speak have an ancient source
and their practice can be mastered,
but they are not understood, so, therefore,
I am not understood.

Those who understand me are rare;
while those who imitate me are acclaimed.

Thus, the Sage wears rudimentary, coarse clothing
and carries what is most precious in his or her heart.

第七十一章
知不知上不知知病夫唯病病是以不
病聖人不病以其病病是以不病

71

Know that You Do Not Know

To know that one does not know
is the highest Insight.

To not know but to think one knows
is an illness.

Recognize this illness as illness,
and one is not ill.

Recognizing that this illness is an illness,
the Sage is not ill.

第七十二章
民不畏威則大威至無狎其所居無厭
其所生夫唯不厭是以不厭是以聖人
自知不自見自愛不自貴故去彼取此

72

Humility

When men have no fear of power,
great power can be had.

Do not encroach into people's homes,
do not despise their existence,
and the people will approve;
thus, there is no disapproval.

The Sages, therefore, know themselves
but do not display themselves;
they respect themselves
but do not glorify themselves;
they give one thing away
and gain another.

第七十三章

勇於敢則殺勇於不敢則活此兩者或利或害天之所惡孰知其故是以聖人猶難之天之道不爭而善勝不言而善應不召而自來繟然而善謀天網恢恢疏而不失

73

Life or Death?

The courageous and reckless
follow killing.

The courageous and prudent
advocate living.

These two positions may be beneficial or harmful.
Who knows what the heavens prefer?
This the Sage, yet, cannot easily answer.

> The Tao does not strive,
> yet it can overcome;
>
> Does not speak,
> yet responds effectively;
>
> Does not appeal for anything,
> yet is supplied naturally;
>
> Desires no result,
> yet has the perfect plan.

Heaven's net is cast wide,
and nothing escapes it.

第七十四章

民不畏死奈何以死懼之若使民常畏
死而為奇者吾得執而殺之孰敢常有
司殺者殺夫代司殺者殺是謂代大匠
斲夫代大匠斲者希有不傷其手矣

74

The Executioner's Dilemma

If people are not afraid to die,
how can they be threatened with death?

If people are made to fear death
and those who do not act properly are executed,
who would dare (do the executing)?

The state has an executioner.

To represent the state as the official executioner can
be called:

> Representing the master carver of wood.

Represent the master carver of wood,
and you rarely escape injury to yourself.

第七十五章

民之饑以其上食稅之多是以饑民之

難治以其上之有為是以難治民之輕

死以其求生之厚是以輕死夫唯無以

生為者是賢於貴生

75

Unconcerned with Death

Taxes imposed by the government are so high
that the people are starving.
And because the people are hungry,
they are difficult to govern.

The authorities have so many schemes and
contrivances
that it makes managing the people difficult.

The people are unconcerned with death.
Their will to live is so great that the fear of death
is faint.

Those who have no fear of death
are able to live a Virtuous and Noble life.

第七十六章

人之生也柔弱其死也堅強萬物草木
之生也柔脆其死也枯槁故堅強者死
之徒柔弱者生之徒是以兵強則不勝
木強則兵強大處下柔弱處上

76

Power of the Supple and Yielding

When people are born,
they are supple and weak.

When people die,
they are hardened and unyielding.

All living creatures, as well as plant life,
are born tender, yielding, delicate.

At death, all are withered and dry.

The hardened and unyielding, therefore,
are disciples of death.

The supple and yielding
are disciples of life.

Thus, a military that is rigid
is bound to fail.

A tree whose wood is strong and hard
falls to the ax.

The strong and powerful
will be subdued.

The supple and yielding
will overcome.

第七十七章

天之道其猶張弓與高者抑之下者舉
之有餘者損之不足者補之天之道損
有餘而補不足人之道則不然損不足
以奉有餘孰能有餘以奉天下唯有道
者是以聖人為而不恃功成而不處其
不欲見賢

77

The Way of Man

The Tao of Heaven
is like a bow being drawn back:

> The high is pulled down
> and the low is pushed up;
>
> The excessive is reduced
> and the insufficient is supplemented.

The Tao of Heaven reduces excess
to make up for that which is deficient.

The way of man is not the same.

Man takes from the needy and indigent
to serve those who have excess.

Who is it that has more than enough
and can offer it all to the world?
The one who possesses the Tao.

Therefore, the Sage works unaided,
accomplishes but needs not be honored.

The Sage has no wish for recognition.

第七十八章

天下莫柔弱於水而攻堅強者莫之能
勝以其無以易之弱之勝強柔之勝剛
天下莫不知莫能行是以聖人云受國
之垢是謂社稷主受國不祥是為天下
王正言若反

78

Truth Seems a Paradox

In all of earthly existence,
none is as supple and submissive as water.
Yet, water can attack and overcome
the solid and strong, without fail.
There is nothing like it.

The weak overcomes the strong
and the supple overcomes the unyielding.

This is known by all under the heavens,
but none put it into practice.

The Sage, therefore, says:

> Those who suffer their nation's humiliation
> are fit to lead.

> Those who suffer their nation's misfortunes
> are fit to oversee all under the heavens.

The truth seems paradoxical.

第七十九章
和大怨必有餘怨安可以為善是以聖
人執左契而不責於人有德司契無德
司徹天道無親常與善人

79

Benevolence

After a bitter quarrel is resolved,
there is certain to remain resentment.

Peace can produce goodwill,
so the Sage, then, keeps his or her word
but does not reproach others for not keeping theirs.

Those of Virtue manage their responsibilities.

Those without Virtue manage to escape their
responsibilities.

The Tao of Heaven is impartial
and always accompanies the benevolent.

第八十章

小國寡民使有什伯之器而不用使民
重死而不遠徙雖有舟輿無所乘之雖
有甲兵無所陳之使人復結繩而用之
甘其食美其服安其居樂其俗鄰國相
望雞犬之聲相聞民至老死不相往來

80

A Community of Contentment

When a country is small,
the population is small.

It is not necessary to create devices
that work ten times more than a single person.

Allow people to value their existent lives
and they will not move away to remote lands.

Though there are boats and carriages,
no one need use them.

Though there are armor and weapons,
no one need display them.

Let the people return to knotting rope, enjoying good food, wearing nice clothing, finding peace in a secure home, and rejoicing in their customs.

Neighboring countries, facing one another, can hear each others' crowing roosters and barking dogs. News is exchanged, yet, the people do not move back and forth. They peaceably grow old and pass on (contented in their own land).

Notes: A society that allows its people to find contentment and joy in their daily lives is a community of people that have no impulse for conflict and aggression with their neighbors.

第八十一章
信言不美美言不信善者不辯辯者不
善知者不博博者不知聖人不積既以
為人己愈有既以與人己愈多天之道
利而不害聖人之道為而不爭

81

Tao of the Sage

Words of Truth are not beautiful.

Beautiful words are not Truth.

The kind are not contentious.

The contentious are not kind.

The Insightful are not those
with extensive knowledge.

Those with extensive knowledge
are not the Insightful.

The Sage does not accumulate.

The more one does for others,
the more one has for oneself.

The more one gives to others,
the more one receives for oneself.

The Tao of Heaven is sharp
but does no harm.

The Tao of the Sage
is to act without striving.

SOURCES

數位經典, http://www.chineseclassic.com/LauTzu/
LaoTzu01.htm (retrieved 08/09/2013)

Alan Chan, *Laozi,* Edward N. Zalta (ed.), The Stanford Encyclopedia of Philosophy (Spring 2014 Edition), http://
plato.stanford.edu/entries/laozi/ (retrieved 01/05/2015)

Arthur Waley, *The Way and its Power: A Study of the Tao Te Ching
and its Place in Chinese Thought* (New York, Grove Press Inc.,1958)

D.C. Lau, *Lao Tzu: Tao Te Ching* (New York, Penguin books,
1963)

John C. H. Wu, *Tao Teh Ching* (Shambhala, 1990)

Lao-tsu translated by Ralph Alan Dale, *Tao Te Ching: A New
Translation and Commentary* (Barnes & Noble Books; 3rd edition,
2004)

Lao-zi translated by Bill Porter, *Lao-tzu's Taoteching* (Copper
Canyon Press; 3rd Revised edition November 1, 2009)

Lao-zi translated by Gia-fu Feng and Jane English, *Lao Tsu: Tao
Te Ching* (New York, Vintage Books, 1989)

Lao-zi translated with annotations by Lok Sang Ho, *The Living
Dao: The Art and Way of Living A Rich & Truthful Life* (Lingnan
University, 2009)

Roger Ames, David Hall, Lao Zi, *Dao De Jing: A Philosophical Translation*, (Ballantine Books, December 30, 2003)

Stephen Mitchell, *Tao Te Ching, Lao Tzu* (Frances Lincoln Limited, 1999)

Thomas Cleary, *The Essential Tao* (Harper San Francisco, 1991)

Ursula K. Le Guin, *Lao Tzu: Tao Te Ching* (Shambhala Publications, 1997)

About the Author

If one points a finger and says, "Look, the moon is beautiful," do you look at the finger or at where the finger is pointing?

Truth and insight, the "moon," are often disregarded and lost when some method, some knowledge, some personality, some dogmatic tradition—the "pointing finger"—is bestowed with undue value and focus and respect. Do not spend your time contemplating and acknowledging the finger.

Where one has been and what one has done, as well as where one plans to go or what one plans to do, is nothing more than a story in one's head. It is all immaterial.

"Do not concentrate on the finger, or you will miss all that heavenly glory."—Bruce Lee

CPSIA information can be obtained
at www.ICGtesting.com
Printed in the USA
LVHW111154290322
714617LV00008B/768